The Magic School Bus

EXPLORES THE WORLD OF BUGS

New York   Toronto   London   Auckland   Sydney
Mexico City   New Delhi   Hong Kong   Buenos Aires

Also look for the Microsoft CD-ROM:
Scholastic's The Magic School Bus Explores the World of Bugs

By Nancy White

Based on *The Magic School Bus* books
written by Joanna Cole and illustrated by Bruce Degen.

ISBN 0-439-22517-5

Illustrated by John Speirs

Cover design by Louise Bova/Interior design by Maria Stasavage

12 11 10 9 8 7 6   3 4 5 6/0

Printed in the U.S.A.   14

First Scholastic printing, October 2001

Our class was making a bug terrarium for the big science fair. Everyone was supposed to catch a live bug and bring it in for the terrarium. But, so far, our project wasn't going very well.

"Well, excuse me, Keesha," said Arnold, "but isn't your caterpillar kind of, well . . . dead?" Arnold's spider was fake, Keesha's caterpillar was dead, and Wanda's ladybug was a windup toy. We just needed insects for the science fair, and then we would let them go. But we hadn't even caught one bug.

What's in *your* bug catcher, Ralphie?

Uh, nothing.

What Is a Bug? (Part One)
by Dorothy Ann

To most people, "bugs" are any tiny creepy-crawly animals—such as:

INSECTS

SPIDERS

WORMS

CENTIPEDES or MILLIPEDES

"Uh-oh. Here comes the Friz," said Carlos. "And she looks like something's bugging her."

"What's this I hear about no bugs?" asked Ms. Frizzle.

"Bugs are creepy and crawly and slimy — yuck!" said Phoebe. "What good are bugs, anyway?"

"I think you'll find some answers on our field trip," said Ms. Frizzle.

Oh boy, a field trip! A change of scene is what we need around here.

Uh-oh. Change is right!

What Is a Bug? (Part Two)
by Dorothy Ann

Scientists use the word "bug" to mean a certain kind of insect—usually one that sucks sap from plants. But even a scientist understands when someone calls a grasshopper or a spider a bug.

BUG?

BUG?

What Is an Insect?
by Carlos

Every insect has six legs and three body parts: head, thorax, and abdomen.

Most insects also have two feelers, or antennae, and two or four wings. An insect's skeleton is on the outside of its body. The skeleton is a hard coat of armor made of chitin—a material a little like your fingernails.

abdomen   thorax   head

5

"Wow, the bus looks just like a bee!" said Phoebe.

"Did I hear the word *bee*?" asked Ms. Frizzle. "Hummmmm — I think that's exactly how we'll start. And if you feel like you're going buggy, Ralphie will signal the bus for a change to a different bug." Then she handed Ralphie a note.

Be a bee!

Tap
Tap
Tap

Dear Ralphie,

When you are a bug, you will have two antennae on your head. Use them to signal the bus for a bug change. Tap your antennae together three times quickly, three times slowly, and three times quickly again.

DON'T FORGET!

Good luck,
Ms. Frizzle

Amazing Antennae
by Keesha

Insects smell with their antennae. They use smell to find places to lay their eggs, to find mates, and to find food. Most insects have a very keen sense of smell. If you leave your garbage can open, a fly can smell it from a mile away. Mmmm, dinner!

The bee-bus landed in a meadow. We were honeybees!

"Where are the boys going?" asked Phoebe.

"To the hive," said D.A. "According to my research, all male bees are *drones*. They are the father bees, and they hang out in the hive a lot."

"I'm glad worker bees are females," said Phoebe. "We get to make the honey."

"Let's get to work," said Wanda. "I hear the nectar is delicious this time of year."

Let's go to the hive.

Have a honey of a time, kids!

Yes. I'm allergic to flowers, anyway.

Social Life
by Phoebe

Bees are known as "social" insects because most kinds of bees live together in groups, or colonies. Honeybees live together in a nest called a hive.

Busy Bees
by Keesha

The female bees are the worker bees. They do all the work in a beehive. They collect nectar and pollen from flowers, feed and care for baby bees, clean the hive, and do repair work.

Recipe for Honey
by Wanda

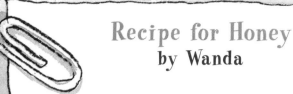

Caution! Don't use this recipe unless you're a bee!

Ingredients:
- nectar (or "juice") from a flower
- chemicals from your stomach

Directions:

1. Suck up nectar from a flower with your long tongue.
2. Store the nectar in your stomach.
3. While you fly back to your hive, the nectar will mix with chemicals in your stomach.
4. Use your mouth to put the nectar in a special compartment in the hive.
5. The nectar will turn into honey.

P.S. You can give some of the nectar to other bees to eat.

"Yum! This nectar is delicious," said Wanda.

"What's this yellow powdery stuff sticking to me?" Phoebe wondered.

"That's pollen," said D.A. "You can use your front legs to brush it into the pollen baskets on your back legs. Then you can carry it back to the hive."

"And when we get back there, we can feed it to the other bees," said Keesha. "They eat a mixture of honey and pollen called *beebread*."

I never knew work could be so much fun.

Life is sweet when you've got flower power!

The Buzz About Pollination
by Dorothy Ann

When bees go from flower to flower looking for nectar, they carry pollen from one flower to another. Many species of flowers need pollen from other flowers of the same species in order to make seeds so that more flowers can grow.

Let's hear it for the bees!

—pollen

In the hive, we met the queen bee. It was Ms. Frizzle! "The queen bee's only job is laying eggs," Queen Friz explained. "The workers feed and take care of her."

"How do you get to be the queen, Ms. Frizzle . . . I mean, Your Majesty?" asked Wanda.

"You have to be chosen when you're just a baby," said Queen Friz.

"I'll never get to be a queen," said Wanda. "Ralphie, please signal to the bus."

Ah . . . this is the life!

Home Sweet Hive
by Ralphie

A beehive is really a nest with lots of storage space. Worker bees shape beeswax into many six-sided compartments called cells. The queen lays eggs in some of the cells. The others are used to store pollen and nectar.

Ouch – That Stings!
by Carlos

People and other animals know to leave a bee alone, because the sting hurts. Only female bees sting. When a honeybee stings, it loses its stinger, and then it dies.

OUCH! STING

Beeswax
by Tim

Young worker bees make a kind of wax in their abdomens. The wax oozes out through tiny holes in the bee's body. The bee chews the wax and then uses it to build parts of the beehive.

At first, we weren't sure Ralphie's signal would work. We waited to see what would happen. Then . . .

"I'm not a bee anymore!" shouted Ralphie, who was now a bright green caterpillar!

"I'm starved," said Keesha, "and leaves make such a lovely lunch."

Just then a beautiful butterfly fluttered by. It was Ms. Frizzle.

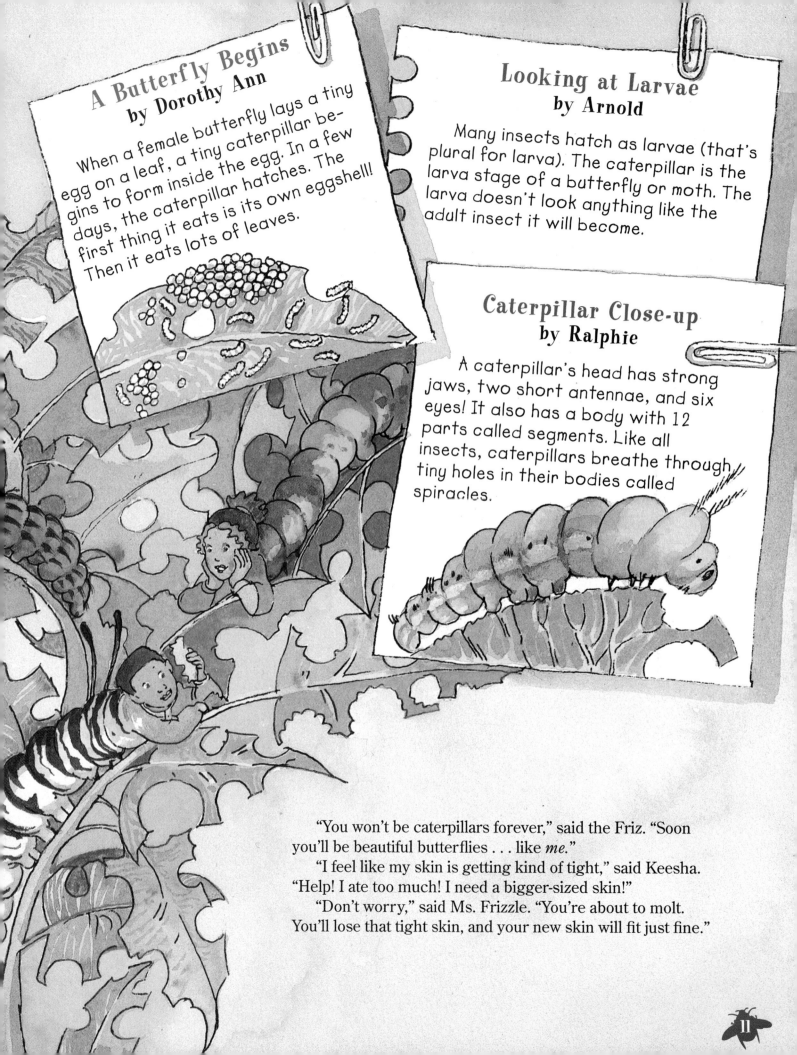

A Butterfly Begins
by Dorothy Ann

When a female butterfly lays a tiny egg on a leaf, a tiny caterpillar begins to form inside the egg. In a few days, the caterpillar hatches. The first thing it eats is its own eggshell! Then it eats lots of leaves.

Looking at Larvae
by Arnold

Many insects hatch as larvae (that's plural for larva). The caterpillar is the larva stage of a butterfly or moth. The larva doesn't look anything like the adult insect it will become.

Caterpillar Close-up
by Ralphie

A caterpillar's head has strong jaws, two short antennae, and six eyes! It also has a body with 12 parts called segments. Like all insects, caterpillars breathe through tiny holes in their bodies called spiracles.

"You won't be caterpillars forever," said the Friz. "Soon you'll be beautiful butterflies . . . like *me*."

"I feel like my skin is getting kind of tight," said Keesha. "Help! I ate too much! I need a bigger-sized skin!"

"Don't worry," said Ms. Frizzle. "You're about to molt. You'll lose that tight skin, and your new skin will fit just fine."

Waiting for Wings
by Wanda

The pupa, or cocoon, stage can last less than ten days, but it usually takes longer. Many kinds of butterflies spend the whole winter in the pupa stage.

Hey, did anybody bring a flashlight?

Wings! I think I'm growing wings!

In my old school, I never turned into a pupa.

Getting Out
by Tim

After the adult butterfly is formed inside the pupa shell, the shell cracks and the butterfly pushes its head out. Next come the legs, and then the rest of the body. It takes only a few minutes.

"What's happening to us?" said Carlos. "This is too weird!"
After we molted, hard shells formed around our bodies. We became very quiet and still. We had entered the pupa stage of life.
As we hung from twigs or leaves, we looked dried up and dead. But inside our shells, our whole bodies were changing. We were turning into beautiful butterflies.

It was awesome being a butterfly.

"What do I look like?" was the first question Wanda asked. "I wish I had a mirror."

We looked so different from when we were caterpillars! Ms. Frizzle took pictures of us so we would be able to see how beautiful we looked.

The Big Change
by Carlos

All the changes – from egg to caterpillar, from pupa to adult butterfly – are called complete metamorphosis. Metamorphosis is just a fancy word for "change." Lots of insects go through these same kinds of changes to become adults.

A Note from the Editors

Dear Readers,

In the real world, different kinds of caterpillars would eat different kinds of leaves. Different kinds of butterflies would not develop in the same place. But in this book, we wanted to show as many different kinds of butterflies as possible. Hope you don't mind!

"I don't like the way those birds are staring at us," said Arnold.

"And that frog," said D.A.

"Butterflies are a very important part of the food chain," Ms. Frizzle explained. "They are a favorite feast for birds, frogs, and lizards. Right, Liz?"

"Look out, Keesha!" shouted D.A., as one of the birds swooped down. Keesha barely escaped being that bird's lunch.

"That's it," said Ralphie, tapping his antennae. "We're out of here."

We knew a change was coming, but what would it be?

Just when we were having so much fun!

Just when we were about to be bird food!

"In my old school, I was afraid of spiders — and now I am one!"

"We're spiderlings!" shouted Tim.

Just a few seconds ago, we had been inside tiny eggs in an egg sac. Now, we were coming out of the egg sac through a little round hole, ready to begin our lives as spiders.

I could grow up to be Spider-Man!

Spiderlings vs. Spiders
by Phoebe

A spiderling is a baby spider. It looks almost like a grown-up spider, only smaller. It will molt a few times as it changes to an adult. But it doesn't completely change, as when a caterpillar turns into a butterfly.

Insects vs. Spiders
by Tim

A spider is NOT an insect. Here is a chart that shows some of the differences between spiders and insects:

BUG	LEGS	WINGS	ANTENNAE	BODY PARTS	EYES
Insects	6	2 or 4	2	3 • head • thorax • abdomen	Most have 2
Spiders	8	0	0	2 • head/thorax combination • abdomen	Most have 8

"Hey, isn't that Ms. Frizzle over there?" asked Phoebe.

"According to my research, she's an orange garden spider," said Dorothy Ann.

"Awesomely accurate," said Ms. Frizzle.

"How did you make that web?" asked Carlos.

Ms. Frizzle told us, "It's just a natural talent I inherited from my family — the group of spiders known as orb weavers."

"Look at that fly," said Tim. "I think he's headed for Ms. Frizzle's web."

Lots of people are afraid of spiders, but only a few spiders have bites that are harmful to people.

Strong Silk
by Phoebe

The silk for a spiderweb starts out as a liquid. It flows out of organs called spinnerets at the rear of the spider's abdomen.

When the liquid hardens into a silk thread, it is stronger than a steel band of the same thickness!

How to Spin a Web
by Ms. Frizzle

1. Make a "bridge" from one tree branch to another.

2. Spin "foundation lines" connecting to lower branches.

"It's Ralphie!" shouted Carlos. "He turned into a fly instead of a spider."

"Lucky for you!" said Ralphie. "Spiders have no antennae. If I had turned into a spider, I wouldn't be able to signal, and you'd be spiders forever."

"I'd stay away from that web if I were you!" warned Carlos.

"Good point!" Ralphie agreed. The next sound we heard was the tapping of his antennae.

Spiders are useful because they eat pesky insects.

I'll try not to take that personally.

Stick to It
by Tim

The solid silk is sticky. Insects that fly into it get trapped – and eaten. The spider doesn't stick to its own web because it has special claws that can hold on to the silk and walk on it.

3. Start spinning threads from the center and going out like the spokes of a wheel.

4. Now that the "frame" for your web is finished, start weaving spiral threads from the center out until you're finished.

How Fireflies Flash
by Keesha

Five different chemicals are stored in a firefly's abdomen. When a sixth chemical is given off, the chemicals light up. To turn off the light, a seventh chemical is added. Whew! It's a regular chemistry lab in there!

I always thought I'd be a star someday!

"Being a spider was fun, class, but now it's time to lighten up," said Ms. Frizzle.
Ralphie tapped, and we were fireflies.
"Are our lights really made of fire?" asked Keesha.
"Our lights are cold — not like fire at all. A firefly could never burn anyone," answered Ms. Frizzle.

Get the Message?
by Arnold

You might think that fireflies light up so that they can see in the dark. But that's not the reason. When a firefly flashes, it's sending a message. It's a firefly's way of attracting a mate.

I never thought I'd be a beetle.

Flashing was fun, but we got worried when Ms. Frizzle warned us that there might be spiderwebs around.

"No one wants to be a spider's midnight snack," she said.

"Uh, Ralphie," said Keesha, "about that signal . . ."

Then we heard Ralphie's *tap, tap, tap*.

This time, we were water boatmen and water striders. The striders were on top of the water, but the boatmen were underwater . . . and upside down!

"Come up, come up, wherever you are," called out Ms. Frizzle. "All you water boatmen have to push the tips of your abdomens above the surface of the water to get air and store it under your wings," called out Ms. Frizzle. "Then, while you're back under the water, you can breathe the air in through your spiracles — those tiny holes in your bodies."

A Note About Prey from Ms. Frizzle

Dear Students,

No matter what kind of insect you are, you'll still have to eat. Some insects, like bees and butterflies, live on pollen or nectar, and some eat plants. But most of them eat other insects — and get eaten themselves.

Frizz

"Stay on your back, use your hind legs like the oars of a row-boat," Ms. Frizzle told us. "Your other legs are for catching and holding your prey."

"Our what?" asked Keesha.

"Prey," Ms. Frizzle repeated. "Your prey is what you hunt and eat — mainly other insects."

"Ugh!" said Keesha.

"RALPHIE . . ." we all called out together.

Ralphie tapped his antennae together.

The Whirligig Beetle
by Tim

The whirligig beetle is an insect that swims on top of the water. Each of this insect's eyes has two parts — one for seeing above the water and the other for seeing under the water.

I'm Superbug!

Anyone want to play hopscotch?

Five-eyed Monsters
by Phoebe

Most insects have two eyes, but a grasshopper has five! It has two big eyes, one small eye on the inside edge of each big eye, and one more small eye near the middle of its face.

"Olympics, here I come," said Tim. "Grasshoppers are the greatest jumpers." We could jump forward 20 times our own length. We could jump upward 10 times our own length. If you could do that as a human, you could leap right over your own house!

"Try rubbing your front wings together," Ms. Frizzle said to Tim.

You should try it, Arnold.

I really wanted to play tuba.

Tim tried what Ms. Frizzle said.

"Tim sounds like he's playing a tiny violin," said Keesha.

"It sounds to me like he needs practice," said Arnold.

"The scientific word for what Tim is doing is *stridulating*," Ms. Frizzle explained. "Male grasshoppers do it to attract females."

Cricket Cousins
by Ralphie

Crickets, locusts, and katydids are close relatives of grasshoppers. These insects can all stridulate, too.

Cricket

Locust

Katydid

"I hate to spoil the fun," said the Friz, "but I should warn you that grasshoppers have many enemies, including the praying mantis."

"And here comes one now," said Phoebe. "Ralphie, get us out of here!"

But Ralphie just froze. He was so scared that he couldn't tap out the signal.

"Everyone stay still," shouted Wanda. "If we don't move, maybe the mantis won't see us."

Growing Grasshoppers
by Arnold

When a baby grasshopper hatches out of its egg, it's not a larva. It's a nymph. It looks almost like an adult, but it has no wings. It gets wings when it grows up.

5 DAYS

20 DAYS

35 DAYS

50 DAYS

Total Destruction
by Wanda

Some grasshoppers can be very destructive. When locusts travel in very large groups they can destroy every plant for miles around. People like praying mantises because they eat grasshoppers and other destructive insects.

24

The Mighty Mantis
by Keesha

When a praying mantis is ready to grab its victim, it darts out its front legs with lightning speed. The sharp hooks on those legs hold the prey in place while the mantis eats it.

The Great Hunter
by Carlos

Praying mantises are made for hunting. Some of them look so much like a leaf that the mantis's prey doesn't see it — until it's too late. And it is the only insect in the world that can turn its head and look over its shoulder — a good skill for a hunter!

"And while we're here," said Ms. Frizzle, "we can learn how the praying mantis got its name. The mantis holds its front legs together as if it were praying, but that is really the mantis's hunting position."

Just in time, Ralphie remembered the signal.

Let's not put one of those in our terrarium.

TAP

TAP

TAP

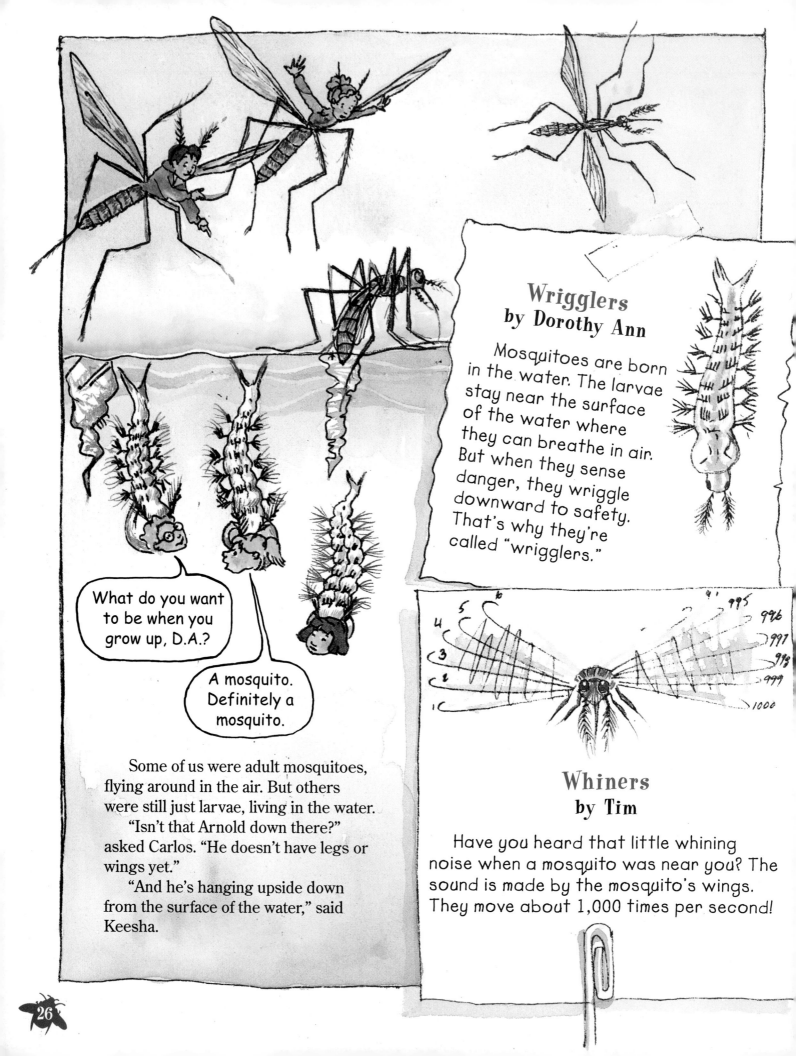

Wrigglers
by Dorothy Ann

Mosquitoes are born in the water. The larvae stay near the surface of the water where they can breathe in air. But when they sense danger, they wriggle downward to safety. That's why they're called "wrigglers."

What do you want to be when you grow up, D.A.?

A mosquito. Definitely a mosquito.

Some of us were adult mosquitoes, flying around in the air. But others were still just larvae, living in the water.

"Isn't that Arnold down there?" asked Carlos. "He doesn't have legs or wings yet."

"And he's hanging upside down from the surface of the water," said Keesha.

Whiners
by Tim

Have you heard that little whining noise when a mosquito was near you? The sound is made by the mosquito's wings. They move about 1,000 times per second!

People blame all mosquitoes for biting, but it's really just the females.

It's not our fault. To lay eggs, we need the protein in animal blood. It's just the way nature made us.

Soon, we were all adults. Each of us had one pair of wings and six legs.

"I once read a book about mosquitoes," said Wanda. "It said that almost all female mosquitoes need blood. They get it from birds, dogs, frogs, and other animals — even humans. Lots of male mosquitoes just eat plant juices."

Mosquito Bites: Part 1
by Wanda

A mosquito can't really bite. Instead, they use their mouths to stab tiny holes in your skin with six needlelike parts called stylets.

Mosquito Bites: Part 2
by Wanda

The mosquito's saliva (or spit) flows into the holes and keeps your blood from clotting while the mosquito sips your blood into its mouth.

Why do mosquito bites itch? Because most people are allergic to mosquitoes' saliva.

"Look at those dragonflies over there," said Wanda.

"They can stand still in the air," Tim noticed. "But when they move, they're really fast."

"I don't like the way they're looking at us," said Arnold. "I can tell they think we're tasty."

Arnold is always such a worrier.

But as the dragonflies flew closer, we realized that they were a lot bigger than we first thought.

The First to Fly
by Carlos

Dragonflies date way back to prehistoric times. There were dragonflies millions of years before there were dinosaurs! They were the first creatures to fly, millions of years before there were any birds.

I think they're pretty.

Yeah, pretty scary.

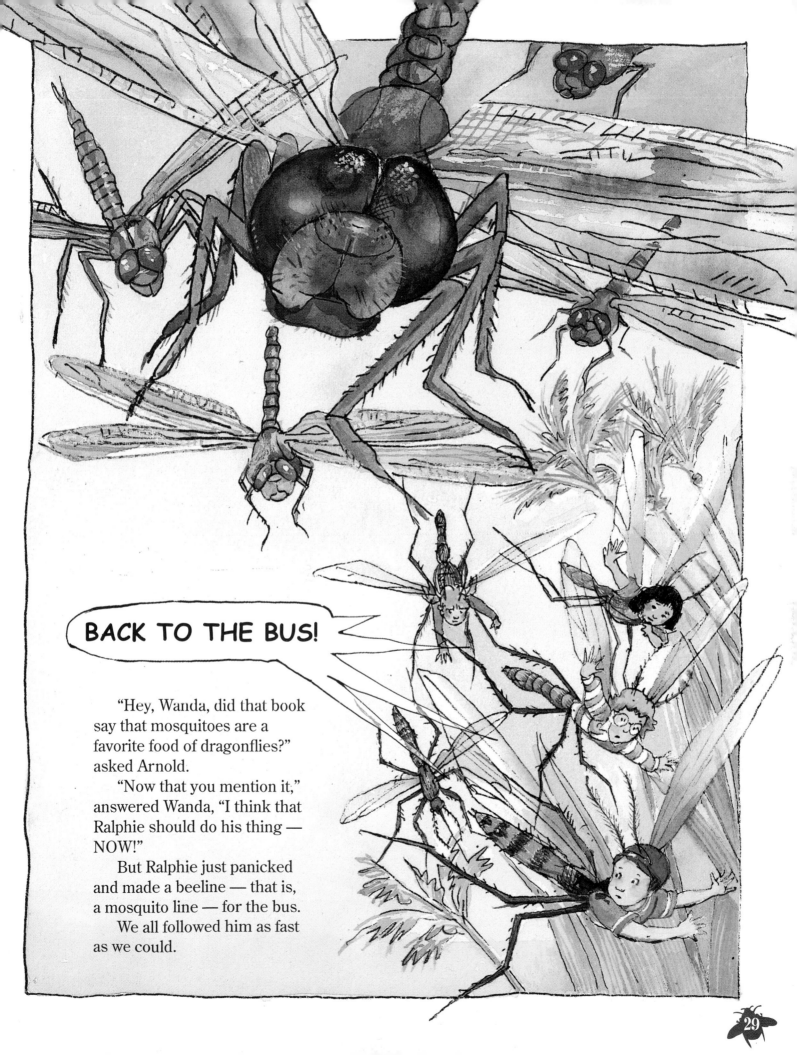

BACK TO THE BUS!

"Hey, Wanda, did that book say that mosquitoes are a favorite food of dragonflies?" asked Arnold.

"Now that you mention it," answered Wanda, "I think that Ralphie should do his thing — NOW!"

But Ralphie just panicked and made a beeline — that is, a mosquito line — for the bus.

We all followed him as fast as we could.

29

Why does some-
body always want
to eat us?

That's life, when
you're an insect!

Thank goodness we reached
the bus just in time.

"Isn't Liz looking at us kind of
funny?" noticed Wanda.

"Oh, dear," said Ms. Frizzle.
"Lizards do love mosquitoes — to
eat, that is."

"No problem!" shouted Ralphie.
Three taps, and . . .

Flying Food
by Tim

Insects are food for many bats,
birds, frogs, lizards, and
even larger animals such as foxes and
monkeys. Without insects,
half the species of birds in the world
would starve.

. . . we were kids again!

"We'll definitely be the bug experts at the science fair," said D.A.

"Oh, no," said Phoebe. "We were so busy *being* bugs, we forgot to *collect* bugs. Our terrarium will be empty."

But when we got back to the classroom, we had a surprise. Liz had been collecting bugs for us. In our terrarium were a bee, a caterpillar, an orange garden spider, a water boatman, a grasshopper, and even a couple of mosquitoes.

"What's that big bug over in the corner?" asked Arnold.

"That's your plastic spider!" said Wanda.

Hooray for Liz!